Our bucket list

1. FIND MY SOUL SISTER(S)

Index

Index

When we decided to do this

_____

BUCKET LIST GOAL

⇩   ⇩

WHY WE WANT TO DO IT

_____
_____
_____
_____

THINGS WE NEED TO PLAN

_____
_____
_____
_____

Date we actually did it

_____

RATING

BEST BITS

_____
_____
_____
_____

Our favourite picture

When we decided to do this

_____

BUCKET LIST GOAL

↓   ↓

WHY WE WANT TO DO IT

_____

_____

_____

_____

THINGS WE NEED TO PLAN

_____

_____

_____

♡

Date we actually did it

_____

RATING

BEST BITS

_____

_____

_____

_____

Our favourite picture

When we decided to do this

_____

BUCKET LIST GOAL

WHY WE WANT TO DO IT

_____

_____

_____

_____

THINGS WE NEED TO PLAN

_____

_____

_____

_____

Date we actually did it

_____

Rating

Best bits

_____
_____
_____
_____

Our favourite picture

When we decided to do this

_____

BUCKET LIST GOAL

WHY WE WANT TO DO IT

_____

_____

_____

_____

THINGS WE NEED TO PLAN

_____

_____

_____

Date we actually did it

_____

Rating

Best bits

_____
_____
_____
_____

Our favourite picture

When we decided to do this

_____

BUCKET LIST GOAL

⇓   ⇓

WHY WE WANT TO DO IT

_____

_____

_____

_____

THINGS WE NEED TO PLAN

_____

_____

_____

♡

Date we actually did it

_____

Rating

Best bits

_____

_____

_____

_____

Our favourite picture

When we decided to do this

_____

BUCKET LIST GOAL

↓   ↓

WHY WE WANT TO DO IT

_____

_____

_____

_____

THINGS WE NEED TO PLAN

_____

_____

_____

_____

♡

Date we actually did it

_____

Rating

Best bits

_____

_____

_____

_____

Our favourite picture

When we decided to do this

_____

BUCKET LIST GOAL

WHY WE WANT TO DO IT

_____
_____
_____
_____

THINGS WE NEED TO PLAN

_____
_____
_____
_____

Date we actually did it

RATING

BEST BITS

_____

_____

_____

_____

Our favourite picture

When we decided to do this

BUCKET LIST GOAL

WHY WE WANT TO DO IT

_____

_____

_____

_____

THINGS WE NEED TO PLAN

_____

_____

_____

_____

Date we actually did it

Rating

BEST BITS

_____

_____

_____

_____

Our favourite picture

When we decided to do this

BUCKET LIST GOAL

↓   ↓

WHY WE WANT TO DO IT

_____

_____

_____

_____

THINGS WE NEED TO PLAN

_____

_____

_____

♡

Date we actually did it

RATING

BEST BITS

_____

_____

_____

_____

Our favourite picture

When we decided to do this

_____

BUCKET LIST GOAL

WHY WE WANT TO DO IT

_____
_____
_____
_____

THINGS WE NEED TO PLAN

_____
_____
_____
_____

Date we actually did it

RATING

Best bits

_____

_____

_____

_____

Our favourite picture

When we decided to do this

_____

BUCKET LIST GOAL

WHY WE WANT TO DO IT

_____

_____

_____

_____

THINGS WE NEED TO PLAN

_____

_____

_____

_____

Date we actually did it

_____

RATING

BEST BITS

_____

_____

_____

_____

Our favourite picture

When we decided to do this

_____

BUCKET LIST GOAL

↓   ↓

WHY WE WANT TO DO IT

_____
_____
_____
_____

THINGS WE NEED TO PLAN

_____
_____
_____
_____

♡

Date we actually did it

_____

RATING

BEST BITS

_____

_____

_____

_____

Our favourite picture

When we decided to do this

_____

BUCKET LIST GOAL

⇩   ⇩

WHY WE WANT TO DO IT

_____

_____

_____

_____

THINGS WE NEED TO PLAN

_____

_____

_____

_____

♡

Date we actually did it

RATING

BEST BITS

_____

_____

_____

_____

Our favourite picture

When we decided to do this

BUCKET LIST GOAL

WHY WE WANT TO DO IT

THINGS WE NEED TO PLAN

♡

Date we actually did it

_____

Rating

Best bits

_____

_____

_____

_____

Our favourite picture

When we decided to do this

_____

BUCKET LIST GOAL

WHY WE WANT TO DO IT

_____

_____

_____

_____

THINGS WE NEED TO PLAN

_____

_____

_____

Date we actually did it

RATING

BEST BITS

_____

_____

_____

_____

Our favourite picture

When we decided to do this

_____

BUCKET LIST GOAL

↓ ↓

WHY WE WANT TO DO IT

_____
_____
_____
_____

THINGS WE NEED TO PLAN

_____
_____
_____

♡

Date we actually did it

_____

Rating

Best bits

_____
_____
_____
_____

Our favourite picture

When we decided to do this

_____

BUCKET LIST GOAL

⇩ ⇩

WHY WE WANT TO DO IT

_____

_____

_____

_____

THINGS WE NEED TO PLAN

_____

_____

_____

_____

♡

Date we actually did it

_____

RATING

BEST BITS

_____

_____

_____

_____

Our favourite picture

When we decided to do this

_____

BUCKET LIST GOAL

WHY WE WANT TO DO IT

_____

_____

_____

THINGS WE NEED TO PLAN

_____

_____

_____

Date we actually did it

_____

Rating

Best bits

_____

_____

_____

_____

Our favourite picture

When we decided to do this

BUCKET LIST GOAL

⇓   ⇓

WHY WE WANT TO DO IT

THINGS WE NEED TO PLAN

♡

Date we actually did it

_____

Rating

Best bits

_____

_____

_____

_____

Our favourite picture

When we decided to do this

_____

BUCKET LIST GOAL

WHY WE WANT TO DO IT

_____

_____

_____

_____

THINGS WE NEED TO PLAN

_____

_____

_____

_____

Date we actually did it

_____

Rating

Best bits

_____

_____

_____

_____

Our favourite picture

When we decided to do this

_____

BUCKET LIST GOAL

WHY WE WANT TO DO IT

_____

_____

_____

_____

THINGS WE NEED TO PLAN

_____

_____

_____

Date we actually did it

_____

RATING

BEST BITS

_____

_____

_____

_____

Our favourite picture

When we decided to do this

_____

BUCKET LIST GOAL

↓   ↓

WHY WE WANT TO DO IT

_____

_____

_____

_____

THINGS WE NEED TO PLAN

_____

_____

_____

♡

Date we actually did it

_____

RATING

BEST BITS

_____

_____

_____

_____

Our favourite picture

When we decided to do this

BUCKET LIST GOAL

↓　　　　　↓

WHY WE WANT TO DO IT

THINGS WE NEED TO PLAN

♡

Date we actually did it

_____

Rating

Best bits

_____

_____

_____

_____

Our favourite picture

When we decided to do this

_____

BUCKET LIST GOAL

↓   ↓

WHY WE WANT TO DO IT

_____

_____

_____

_____

THINGS WE NEED TO PLAN

_____

_____

_____

♡

Date we actually did it

_____

Rating

Best bits

_____

_____

_____

_____

Our favourite picture

When we decided to do this

_____

BUCKET LIST GOAL

↓   ↓

WHY WE WANT TO DO IT

_____

_____

_____

_____

THINGS WE NEED TO PLAN

_____

_____

_____

♡

Date we actually did it

_____

Rating

Best bits

_____
_____
_____
_____

Our favourite picture

When we decided to do this

_____

BUCKET LIST GOAL

↓   ↓

WHY WE WANT TO DO IT

_____

_____

_____

_____

THINGS WE NEED TO PLAN

_____

_____

_____

♡

Date we actually did it

_____

Rating

Best bits

_____

_____

_____

_____

Our favourite picture

When we decided to do this

_____

BUCKET LIST GOAL

⬇   ⬇

WHY WE WANT TO DO IT

_____

_____

_____

_____

THINGS WE NEED TO PLAN

_____

_____

_____

♡

Date we actually did it

_____

Rating

Best bits

_____

_____

_____

_____

Our favourite picture

When we decided to do this

_____

BUCKET LIST GOAL

WHY WE WANT TO DO IT

_____

_____

_____

_____

THINGS WE NEED TO PLAN

_____

_____

_____

_____

Date we actually did it

_____

RATING

BEST BITS

_____
_____
_____
_____

Our favourite picture

When we decided to do this

_____

BUCKET LIST GOAL

WHY WE WANT TO DO IT

_____

_____

_____

THINGS WE NEED TO PLAN

_____

_____

_____

Date we actually did it

_____

Rating

Best bits

_____

_____

_____

_____

Our favourite picture

When we decided to do this

_____

BUCKET LIST GOAL

↓   ↓

WHY WE WANT TO DO IT

_____

_____

_____

_____

THINGS WE NEED TO PLAN

_____

_____

_____

♡

Date we actually did it

_____

Rating

Best bits

_____

_____

_____

_____

Our favourite picture

When we decided to do this

_____

BUCKET LIST GOAL

WHY WE WANT TO DO IT

_____

_____

_____

_____

THINGS WE NEED TO PLAN

_____

_____

_____

_____

Date we actually did it

_____

Rating

Best bits

_____

_____

_____

_____

Our favourite picture

When we decided to do this

_____

BUCKET LIST GOAL

↓   ↓

WHY WE WANT TO DO IT

_____

_____

_____

_____

THINGS WE NEED TO PLAN

_____

_____

_____

_____

♡

Date we actually did it

Rating

Best bits

_____

_____

_____

_____

Our favourite picture

When we decided to do this

_____

BUCKET LIST GOAL

↓   ↓

WHY WE WANT TO DO IT

_____

_____

_____

_____

THINGS WE NEED TO PLAN

_____

_____

_____

♡

Date we actually did it

_____

RATING

BEST BITS

_____

_____

_____

_____

Our favourite picture

When we decided to do this

BUCKET LIST GOAL

↓   ↓

WHY WE WANT TO DO IT

THINGS WE NEED TO PLAN

Date we actually did it

_____

Rating

Best bits

_____

_____

_____

_____

Our favourite picture

When we decided to do this

_____

BUCKET LIST GOAL

WHY WE WANT TO DO IT

_____

_____

_____

_____

THINGS WE NEED TO PLAN

_____

_____

_____

_____

Date we actually did it

_____

Rating

Best bits

_____

_____

_____

_____

Our favourite picture

When we decided to do this

_____

BUCKET LIST GOAL

WHY WE WANT TO DO IT

_____

_____

_____

_____

THINGS WE NEED TO PLAN

_____

_____

_____

_____

Date we actually did it

_____

RATING

BEST BITS

_____
_____
_____
_____

Our favourite picture

When we decided to do this

_____

BUCKET LIST GOAL

WHY WE WANT TO DO IT

_____
_____
_____
_____

THINGS WE NEED TO PLAN

_____
_____
_____
_____

Date we actually did it

_____

Rating

Best bits

_____

_____

_____

_____

Our favourite picture

When we decided to do this

BUCKET LIST GOAL

WHY WE WANT TO DO IT

_____

_____

_____

_____

THINGS WE NEED TO PLAN

_____

_____

_____

_____

Date we actually did it

_____

Rating

Best bits

_____

_____

_____

_____

Our favourite picture

When we decided to do this

_____

BUCKET LIST GOAL

↓   ↓

WHY WE WANT TO DO IT

_____

_____

_____

_____

THINGS WE NEED TO PLAN

_____

_____

_____

♡

Date we actually did it

Rating

Best bits

Our favourite picture

When we decided to do this

_____

BUCKET LIST GOAL

WHY WE WANT TO DO IT

_____

_____

_____

_____

THINGS WE NEED TO PLAN

_____

_____

_____

_____

Date we actually did it

_____

RATING

BEST BITS

_____

_____

_____

_____

Our favourite picture

When we decided to do this

_____

BUCKET LIST GOAL

↓   ↓

WHY WE WANT TO DO IT

_____

_____

_____

_____

THINGS WE NEED TO PLAN

_____

_____

_____

_____

♡

Date we actually did it

_____

Rating

Best bits

_____
_____
_____
_____

Our favourite picture

When we decided to do this

_____

BUCKET LIST GOAL

WHY WE WANT TO DO IT

_____

_____

_____

_____

THINGS WE NEED TO PLAN

_____

_____

_____

_____

Date we actually did it

RATING

BEST BITS

_____

_____

_____

_____

Our favourite picture

When we decided to do this

_____

BUCKET LIST GOAL

WHY WE WANT TO DO IT

_____

_____

_____

_____

THINGS WE NEED TO PLAN

_____

_____

_____

_____

Date we actually did it

_____

Rating

⭐1 ⭐2 ⭐3 ⭐4 ⭐5

Best bits

_____

_____

_____

_____

Our favourite picture

When we decided to do this

_____

BUCKET LIST GOAL

WHY WE WANT TO DO IT

_____

_____

_____

_____

THINGS WE NEED TO PLAN

_____

_____

_____

_____

Date we actually did it

_____

Rating

Best bits

_____

_____

_____

_____

Our favourite picture

When we decided to do this

_____

BUCKET LIST GOAL

WHY WE WANT TO DO IT

_____

_____

_____

_____

THINGS WE NEED TO PLAN

_____

_____

_____

_____

Date we actually did it

RATING

BEST BITS

Our favourite picture

When we decided to do this

_____

BUCKET LIST GOAL

WHY WE WANT TO DO IT

_____

_____

_____

_____

THINGS WE NEED TO PLAN

_____

_____

_____

_____

Date we actually did it

_____

Rating

Best bits

_____

_____

_____

_____

Our favourite picture

When we decided to do this

_____

| BUCKET LIST GOAL |

↓   ↓

WHY WE WANT TO DO IT

_____

_____

_____

_____

THINGS WE NEED TO PLAN

_____

_____

_____

_____

♡

Date we actually did it

_____

Rating

Best bits

_____
_____
_____
_____

Our favourite picture

When we decided to do this

BUCKET LIST GOAL

↓   ↓

WHY WE WANT TO DO IT

_____

_____

_____

_____

THINGS WE NEED TO PLAN

_____

_____

_____

_____

♡

Date we actually did it

_____

Rating

Best bits

_____
_____
_____
_____

Our favourite picture

When we decided to do this

_____

BUCKET LIST GOAL

↓   ↓

WHY WE WANT TO DO IT

_____
_____
_____
_____

THINGS WE NEED TO PLAN

_____
_____
_____

♡

Date we actually did it

_____

Rating

Best bits

_____

_____

_____

_____

Our favourite picture

When we decided to do this

_____

BUCKET LIST GOAL

WHY WE WANT TO DO IT

_____
_____
_____
_____

THINGS WE NEED TO PLAN

_____
_____
_____
_____

Date we actually did it

_____

Rating

Best bits

_____
_____
_____
_____

Our favourite picture

Made in United States
Troutdale, OR
08/12/2023

12016395R00060